What's So Great About Benjamin Franklin?

A Biography of Benjamin Franklin Just for Kids!

Max Tanner

KidLit-O Books
www.kidlito.com

© 2014. All Rights Reserved.

Table of Contents

About KidCaps

KidLit-O is an imprint of BookCaps™ that is just for kids! Each month BookCaps will be releasing several books in this exciting imprint. Visit are website or like us on Facebook to see more!

To add your name to our mailing list, visit this link: **http://www.kidlito.com/mailing-list.html**

Introduction

The sixteen year old boy snapped his head up at the sound. Was it his imagination or was there someone standing outside his door? Tucking a pile of papers into a drawer, young Benjamin Franklin stood up from his writing desk and walked over to the locked door. He opened it a crack and saw the sneering face of his older brother, James.

"What are you doing, brother? Why have you locked yourself away in here all evening? You have ink on your hand. Have you been writing?"

Benjamin looked his brother in the eye with a slight smile. "Oh, you know," he said. "I am not doing anything of importance. I was just scribbling down some of my thoughts."

James shook his head. "Benjamin, when will you learn that life is too short to be wasted locking oneself away and writing words that no one will ever read or care about?" With a final sneer, James turned on his heel and walked back down the hall, leaving Benjamin standing alone in the doorway.

Benjamin smiled, closed the door, and walked back to his desk. After pulling out the papers he had stuffed into the drawer, he sat back down and lifted the quill from its holder. He thought out loud: "Where was I? Ah yes…

"Sir, it may not be improper in the first Place to inform your Readers, that I intend once a Fortnight to present them, by the Help of this Paper, with a short Epistle, which I presume will add somewhat to their Entertainment."[2]

The letters flowed from his quill and Benjamin organized his thoughts and made sure to choose the most powerful words to make his point. Once he finished the letter, he signed the name "Silence Dogood" at the bottom. Tonight, he would slip this letter under the door of James' newspaper, and then the whole community of Boston would read the words Benjamin had written this day. No one would know that the well-spoken widow writing about serious issues of the day was actually a teenaged boy. But perhaps even if they did know it might not change their opinion. Benjamin was sure that the writing was good and that the arguments were valid.

Young Benjamin Franklin chuckled to himself as he slipped the completed letter back into the drawer. His brother James had said that no one would ever read what Benjamin had been writing up here. Little did James know that it was his very own printing press that would print Benjamin's words for the world to both read and care about.

From a remarkably young age, Benjamin Franklin was different than the other children. Instead of just playing games, he used his mind to interact with the world around him and to do things that had never been done before.

[2] Quotation: http://en.wikipedia.org/wiki/Silence_Dogood

Throughout his life, he would use his words to change the opinions of entire nations, and would use his imagination to make his environment a better place. For good reason, many people call Benjamin Franklin "The First American". Not only was he alive when the United States won its independence from England, but he was also one of the first people to live up to the ideals that the nation was founded on. He used his freedom to build up his community and to benefit the whole world.

Benjamin Franklin was one of the Founding Fathers of the United States. Many of his ideas were included in both the Declaration of Independence and the US Constitution of 1787. To this day, Benjamin Franklin has remained a cherished figure in American history.

It can be hard to define exactly what kind of person Benjamin Franklin was, if only because he seemed to do everything and be everywhere at the same time. He was a prolific writer, a businessman, a real estate baron, a politician, a community leader, an inventor, a scientist… and the list goes on. He established the first library and volunteer fire department in the New World and served as a soldier in the Pennsylvania colony's militia. He encouraged people to do good things for others without asking anything in return and helped to oversee the nation's postal routes.

Even though he tried so many new things, Benjamin Franklin wasn't afraid to fail. Along with his many successes, Benjamin also met with many failures. He once wrote:

"Do not fear mistakes. You will know failure. Continue to reach out."[3]

He followed his own advice. Although he was able to run more than one successful publication, he also tried to start a magazine that no one wanted to read and to redesign the English alphabet that no one thought needed redesigning. But occasional failure didn't stop Benjamin Franklin.

Ever the tireless worker, this "First American" always tried to find practical solutions to the problems of his day - whether those problems were political or scientific in nature, or even had to do with keeping his fellow colonists warm in the middle of a snowy winter.

Even though more than 200 years have passed since this brilliant man died, his presence is still felt every day in the United States. The words that he wrote during his lifetime have been repeated thousands of times over, and they still guide and teach Americans valuable lessons all these years later. Here are a few of Franklin's well-known quotations:

"Remember that time is money."
"Those who would give up essential Liberty, to purchase a little temporary Safety, deserve neither Liberty nor Safety."

---

[3]   Quote:
http://www.brainyquote.com/quotes/quotes/b/benjaminfr119119.html

"It is better 100 guilty Persons should escape than that one innocent Person should suffer."
"An ounce of prevention is worth a pound of cure."[4]

Benjamin Franklin was born in extraordinary times. The people of the thirteen colonies were considering rebelling against their English masters, and each person would be forced to choose where they would stand on the issue of independence. The young nation would need brave men and women to stand up to tyranny and take the lead, helping others on the path to liberty and freedom.

Benjamin Franklin was one of those people.

His path to greatness began when he was just a boy working alongside his brother in a print shop.

---

[4] Quotations: http://en.wikiquote.org/wiki/Benjamin_Franklin

Chapter 1: Benjamin Franklin's Early Life and Education

Back in the days when Benjamin Franklin was born, it wasn't uncommon for parents to have a lot of kids. Ben Franklin's father, named Josiah, had a total of 17 children with two different wives. Can you imagine what it would have been like to have so many brothers and sisters? What would family meals have been like?

Ben was the tenth and final son of Josiah, and the fifteenth overall of the seventeen children. His mother's, Abiah, was Josiah's second wife. She ended up having ten of his children, which meant that Benjamin had nine full brothers and sisters and seven half brothers and sisters. Abiah gave birth to Benjamin on January 17, 1706, in the city of Boston, Massachusetts.

Back then, Boston was part of an English colony, and everyone who was born in Boston was considered a citizen of the British Empire. As he grew up, Benjamin Franklin would be very proud to be a part of the British Empire, with its advanced culture, strong economy, and dry sense of humor.

As you can probably imagine, there was a lot of work to be done in the Franklin family – after all there were so many Franklins running around! There was cooking and cleaning to do, the boys had to become apprentices and learn a trade, and there were of course many happy nights spent together as a family.

By the time young Benjamin was born some of his brothers and sisters were already adults. Many had already chosen what careers they wanted to learn while others of them had their father choose their careers for them. Josiah Franklin worked hard to provide for his family as a soap and candle maker. He was proud of his humble job and taught his children the value of hard work and getting the job done right. But Josiah recognized the intelligence of his young son Benjamin and thought that perhaps he could do a more good for the community if he was trained as a member of the clergy as religious teachers are sometimes called.

Even though Benjamin did well in school, and probably could have made his father's dream come true if he had been given the chance, times got pretty tough in the Franklin household, and Benjamin wasn't able to finish his training to become a religious teacher. After just a few years of school, when he was 10 years old, his father asked him to stop his studies and to work full-time with him making candles and bars of soap.

Benjamin was an obedient son and happily went to work with his father. He did excellent work, too. He was good with his hands and paid lots of attention to detail, but even so it soon became clear that Benjamin was not very satisfied with life as a candle maker - he was getting bored. Cutting string for wicks and dipping candles in tubs of hot wax was not particularly exciting or challenging work for Benjamin's active mind.

It seems that his father Josiah noticed that Benjamin's growing boredom with the job. Since one of Josiah's older sons had left home to work on a boat – against his father's wishes – Josiah was worried that Benjamin's boredom might make him do something just as dangerous, taking him far away from his home and family. So when Benjamin was twelve years old and had spent about two years making candles with his father, Josiah sent him to work as an apprentice with his older brother James Franklin.

5 Image: http://www.ushistory.org/franklin/temple/single.htm

Ben's brother James had the first newspaper in New England that printed local stories. Although two other newspapers were printed in the New England area, those papers only reported things that had already been reported in English newspapers overseas – they didn't pay any attention to the things happening in Boston and didn't talk about the things that interested the people who lived there. Recognizing that people would like to read stories about people and places they saw every day, James and his friends started a paper and called it *The New England Courant*. James and his friends and wrote the majority of the articles themselves.

Young Benjamin really liked working at the print shop. Even though he was still a boy – only twelve years old - he proved himself to be a hard worker. But unlike his time at as a candle maker, Benjamin was fascinated and motivated to do a good job as a printer. After working long hours to set all of the letters in just the right positions on the printer - so that the final product would look right - Benjamin would go outside and sell the pamphlets and papers himself to passersby on the street. He would shout out the contents of the printed material and how much each pamphlet or paper cost. Sometimes he would take advantage of catchy headlines to sell more.

By the time he was sixteen, Benjamin felt pretty comfortable working as a printer and salesman. He felt that he could do more than just print and sell papers – he felt that he was ready to write some of the content. But when he spoke to his brother James, who was one of the editors of the paper, he was told that no one would ever take the paper seriously if there was a child writing some of the articles. It can be hard sometimes for older siblings to see their younger siblings as anything but little kids.

Of course, James' words stung Benjamin. But instead of getting angry and picking a fight, Benjamin decided to prove his talent in an interesting way – he decided to write articles and submit them to the paper under a "pen name", or a false name. That way, everyone would focus on the words and not on the author. Then maybe his brother James would see that Benjamin should be given more responsibility.

Benjamin slipped the first of the letters signed by an old widow named "Silence Dogood" under the door of the print shop one night, and soon he saw that very letter in the pages of *The New England Courant*.

The letters "Silence Dogood" wrote spoke about some of the problems in Boston, and those who read the letters loved them. The letters said the very things that many people had been thinking, and it wasn't long before everyone was trying to figure out who this mysterious "Silence Dogood" actually was.

[6]

Image:
http://www.masshist.org/database/images/4795nec17220910_a_1_ref.jpg

Young Benjamin went on to write a whole series of letters before it was discovered that he, and not an educated widow, was actually their author. While most people were amused at the lengths that young Benjamin had gone to in order to prove his point, his older brother James was not amused. In fact, James was kind of jealous that Benjamin had gotten so much attention and was angry that his little brother had embarrassed him in such a public way.

A short time later, James was put into jail for a few months after he angered a powerful Puritan family with some things that he published in his paper. Benjamin was left all alone to run the paper, and he actually did a pretty good job. But when James got out of jail, instead of being impressed by Benjamin's business skills and giving him more responsibility, he was as mean to his little brother as ever.

Knowing that he could never get ahead while working as an apprentice to James, Benjamin Franklin did something illegal – he ran away from home at the age of 15. He knew that his future lay outside of Boston.

It was against the law for a young boy to wander the streets away from home and to be without an apprenticeship. Benjamin knew that he could probably get a job working in a print shop somewhere, so for the next two years he wandered around New England looking for steady work. He started with New York City, but things didn't go too well for him there. So he decided to go across the Hudson River to New Jersey. He didn't have much success in New Jersey either, so he travelled a little further on until he came to Philadelphia.

It was in the city of Philadelphia that things looked their darkest for young Benjamin. He didn't have a job or a permanent place to stay, and he had just spent the last of his money on some bread to eat. Soaked by the rain, it's safe to say that no one expected anything great to come from this poor child, now seventeen years old.

Benjamin Franklin had nowhere to go and nothing to do.

It may have seemed like a miracle when, on October 6, 1723, Benjamin first met the Read family. Although he probably looked pretty pitiful, wet and lonely and with no money, The Reads gave Benjamin food and a place to sleep, and he was grateful. But it was the Read family's daughter, Deborah, that most interested Benjamin. She was beautiful, intelligent, and charming.

Sometime after meeting with the Reads, Deborah expressed some interest in marrying Benjamin, but he thought that he wasn't ready yet. He thought that he needed more stability in his life and needed to grow up a little.

In the meantime, Benjamin earned himself the same reputation that he had earned back in Boston – that of a hard worker. He obtained government contracts for the print shop and eventually met the Governor of Pennsylvania, William Keith, who extended a very special invitation to him. The Governor invited Benjamin to sail to England to pick up some special printing supplies. If he did so, the Governor would help Benjamin to set up a printing shop of his own. He promised to send some letters of recommendation that would make it easier for Benjamin to get what he needed.

Benjamin immediately set sail for London, but unfortunately the Governor didn't keep his word and the letters he had promised never arrived. Benjamin, by this time about 20 years old, was left to fend for himself in London. But being such a capable worker, he was soon able to find a job in a print shop. It was in London where Benjamin was able to write and publish his first pamphlet "*A Dissertation upon Liberty and Necessity, Pleasure and Pain.*"

For the almost three years that he spent in London, Benjamin Franklin enjoyed as much of English culture as he could. After each workday ended, he savored deep philosophical conversations over cups of coffee and listened to funny men tell funny stories. He attended well-written and performed plays and concerts and generally just soaked in a rich culture that he felt the colonies were missing. Franklin truly enjoyed his life as a subject of the English crown and couldn't ever imagine that his opinion about that would change one day.

Even though he was happy in London, it wasn't long before Benjamin began to think about the city that he had left behind – Philadelphia. Although he had been born and raised in Boston, he had come to think of Philadelphia – "the city of brotherly love" – as his new home.

By 1729, Benjamin Franklin had made the long trip back to Philadelphia and was looking for a way to get back into the printing industry. He started working again as a printer's apprentice and soon got government contracts. But his chance to break out on his own came when he got the opportunity to purchase a newspaper called *The Pennsylvania Gazette*. That's how Benjamin found himself in the same position as his big brother James had been in before – he was the owner and editor of a newspaper.

But this time, there would be no one to tell him what he could and could not do with it. He wouldn't be told that he was too young to write because he would be the editor to make those decisions. He would be sure to add as much content as he wanted to it. In fact, Franklin himself drew the paper's first political cartoon.

At 23 years old, Benjamin Franklin had established himself as a serious man who knew how to work. Even though he was still quite young, he had already become the owner of a progressive newspaper that gave the people what they wanted - local news and juicy gossip. He had travelled to the other side of the Atlantic Ocean and published his thoughts in a well-received pamphlet. In fact, Benjamin wrote a second pamphlet and published it around this time. It was titled "*Articles of Belief and Acts of Religion*", and like his first pamphlet which talked about his views on God and his place in everyday life, the second one was also well-received by those who read it.

The conditions were just about right for Benjamin Franklin to start doing incredible things. His finances were secure, and he had the respect of the community. The words he wrote were taken seriously and - being aware of the fact that he was living in momentous times - he used those words to help other people to think about serious issues. Franklin's mind had a marvellous way of finding practical solutions to complex problems, and for every problem that he saw Franklin would try to find a simple and reasonable solution for it.

Shortly after purchasing *The Pennsylvania Gazette*, Benjamin Franklin started the first of many projects to improve the lives of the people around him. His time in England had showed him the good things that could come from people working together to make the community a better place. In 1729, at the age of 23, Franklin started his first social club to try and make a difference.

Chapter 2: The Career of Benjamin Franklin

The first major step that Benjamin Franklin took to improve his community was starting a social club for the young men who lived in Philadelphia. Called the Junto, the club was a place where young men could get together to talk about the problems they saw in the community and was a place to develop the skills and abilities they needed to have in order to take on a bigger role in society. In their own words, the club was for "self-improvement, study, mutual aid, and conviviality".[7]

The Junto let Benjamin Franklin and his friends put their heads (and wallets) together to improve the city of Philadelphia. In fact, some of the ideas that these young men came up with would later spread to other parts of the colonies and even the world, helping hundreds of thousands of people down through the years. What were some of the ideas that Benjamin Franklin came up with during this time?

Perhaps one of the most influential ideas was a subscription library. Knowing that most people in the city of Philadelphia were too poor to buy and keep large collections of books in their homes, Benjamin Franklin and his friends decided to pool their money

[7] Quote: http://www.ushistory.org/franklin/info/timeline.htm

to buy books. Then, they made these books available to anyone who could pay a small monthly subscription fee. The money that came in each month from the subscriptions was then used to buy even more books and to make the library better and better. Thus, the community had a library which was always stocked with the most useful and up-to-date books.

It was especially from 1730 to 1740 that Benjamin Franklin and his associates focused on making Philadelphia one of the best cities in the world. For example, they spoke to the city government and asked that the streets be made safer and more comfortable. What were the results? The government installed more lights that made the road easier to see at night, and muddy streets were soon paved over. The government also ensured that there was a system in place to clean the streets on a regular basis, which had the double effect of making the city look nicer and helping to prevent diseases from spreading.

Thanks in large part to Benjamin Franklin, the city of Philadelphia saw lots of improvements. In addition to seeing the city that he loved doing very well, Franklin's business life was also going very well. Aside from *The Pennsylvania Gazette*, which he continued to publish and write for, Benjamin had started to publish an annual book called *Poor Richard's Almanack*. Writing as if he were a simple farmer, the book gave weather and farming advice for the coming year and included lots of humor and practical wisdom.

Poor Richard's Almanack gave Benjamin Franklin a chance to share some of his wonderful and charming personality with all Thirteen Colonies. He used his wit and intelligence to shape the thinking of average Americans, teaching them to be more responsible with their time and money and making sure that they thought ahead about the consequences of their actions. In other words, he gave advice to his fellow Americans like a loving father would to his children.

Poor Richard, 1733.

A N

Almanack

For the Year of Chrift

1733,

Being the Firft after LEAP YEAR:

And makes fince the Creation	Years
By the Account of the Eastern *Greeks*	7241
By the Latin Church, when ☉ ent. ♈	6932
By the Computation of *W. W.*	5742
By the *Roman* Chronology	5682
By the *Jewish* Rabbies	5494

Wherein is contained

The Lunations, Eclipfes, Judgment of the Weather, Spring Tides, Planets Motions & mutual Afpects, Sun and Moon's Rifing and Setting, Length of Days, Time of High Water, Fairs, Courts, and obfervable Days.

Fitted to the Latitude of Forty Degrees, and a Meridian of Five Hours Weft from *London*, but may without fenfible Error, ferve all the adjacent Places, even from *Newfoundland* to *South-Carolina.*

By *RICHARD SAUNDERS*, Philom.

PHILADELPHIA:
Printed and fold by *B. FRANKLIN*, at the New Printing-Office near the Market.

It was around this time that something very special happened in Benjamin Franklin's private life– he finally found love.

While Benjamin was away in England, Deborah Read (the young girl that he had developed a crush on as a young man) had been given away in marriage to a man named John Rogers. But Rogers wasn't really a nice guy and, in fact, ended up stealing a slave and then running away to avoid getting caught and put in jail. Rogers escaped to the Caribbean and never came back.

Even though Deborah was sad that her husband had run away and abandoned her, she was happy that, after so many years, she could finally start a relationship with Benjamin. Benjamin was about 24 years old by then and had become successful with both his business and charitable rojects.

Because Deborah couldn't get a certificate of divorce from her first husband (he was living far away in Barbados, and there wasn't any email back then) she and Benjamin could never get legally married. But they did live together for 44 years until she died in 1774. During that time, they had what was called a "common-law marriage. In other words, even though they couldn't get a piece of paper to show that they were legally married, everyone knew how much Benjamin and Deborah loved each other and that they were absolutely devoted to their relationship.

[8] Image: http://library.thinkquest.org/22254/3.gif

Now that he was with Deborah, Benjamin's personal life saw even more big changes. Back when he was 22, he had fathered a child with another girl, but now he and Deborah officially adopted the child named William and raised him together. Later, Benjamin and Deborah had two children of their own, a boy and a girl. Sadly, the boy Francis died when he was just 4 years old after contracting smallpox. But their daughter Sally lived a long life and ended up taking care of her dear father in his old age until the day he died.

As his family and businesses grew, Benjamin developed an admirable philosophy of "paying it forward". In other words, whenever things went well for him he tried to make sure that things went well for others too. Because his personal and professional lives were making him so happy, Benjamin wanted to make the lives of those around him happy, as well.

In 1736, Benjamin addressed a vital need in Philadelphia – there weren't any firefighters. Back when most houses were made of wood and often built close together, a single large fire could destroy an entire neighborhood block or even a large city. So a good idea to prevent his from happening would be to have a team of men ready to leap into action at any minute in case a fire broke out and to keep it from spreading. Benjamin Franklin started the Philadelphia Union Fire Company of volunteer firefighters in 1736 and the idea quickly spread to other cities.

Although there were expenses involved in purchasing equipment and time was needed to train the firefighters, Benjamin Franklin said "An ounce of prevention is worth a pound of cure." In other words, it would be better to spend a little time and money establishing a fire department than spending lots of time and money later on rebuilding burnt and destroyed homes.

A few years later, Franklin also took steps to help the victims of house fires. Some families who lost their homes and possessions in a fire felt absolutely ruined, with no money to start their lives over again. Seeing this sad situation, Franklin decided to start a fire insurance program to help poor families get back on their feet after having lost their homes in a fire.

Benjamin also decided to map out the different postal routes and help the mail move faster and more efficiently from one place to another. For his hard work in this area, he was appointed as the British Postmaster, something that let him set up communication routes that would later be used during the Revolution.

By 1748, Benjamin Franklin was in a pretty strong position, financially speaking. He had more money than he needed. His family was happy and healthy, his two kids were 21 and 6 respectively, so it was in this year the Benjamin decided to sell both of his successful publications: *Poor Richard's Almanack* and *The Pennsylvania Gazette*.

Knowing that the colonies around him still had a lot of improvements that needed to be made, Franklin decided to retire from working the following year at the age of 42. He organized the Pennsylvania militia in 1756 so that there would be a constant organization to protect and defend his colony. Then, he decided to see if he could help even more people.

Although he loved hard work, Franklin felt that his talents would be better used if he worked as a scientist and inventor, trying to learn more about the natural world and using what he learned to help his fellow man. He had enjoyed some success a few years earlier when he invented the Franklin stove, a new type of wood burning stove that produced more heat and less smoke. It allowed families that used to be cold during the long winter months to stay warmer, happier, and healthier. Because his stove was meant to improve the common good of man, Franklin refused to patent it and to make himself rich.

So when Franklin finally made the decision to become an inventor, it wasn't money that motivated him – it was more important for him to keep on learning and helping others.

As a scientist, Benjamin chose not to focus on just one area - he spent time studying anything and everything that he found interesting, and that might be able to help the world.

For example, very impressed with the power of lightning, Franklin wondered if the small sparks of static electricity he felt and the huge bolts of lightning he saw in the sky might be the same thing. So he started doing several experiments during thunderstorms. Ben Franklin figured that if lightning and electricity were related then he should be able to capture some electricity from the air during a lightning storm and store it in a special jar that could act like a battery.

On one stormy day in 1752, Ben Franklin went outside with his son William to test out his theory. He flew a kite with a silk string and tied a metal key to the bottom of the string. Then he placed a small piece of metal wire to connect the key to a nail in the top of a special battery jar. As the thunderstorm moved closer and static electricity began to fill the air, Benjamin Franklin went into a nearby barn with his son. After the storm had passed, Ben Franklin moved his hand near the key and felt a shock. He was excited at the results of his experiment.

Electricity from the air during the storm had travelled down the string to the key and was then collected into the jar. It was this stored electricity that had given Ben Franklin a shock when he got too close to it. Ben Franklin had just proved that lightning was actually a

9   Image: http://media-1.web.britannica.com/eb-media/27/8427-004-0CA75BD2.jpg

form of electricity. He would later be the first to explain that electricity could have either a positive or a negative charge, a discovery that would help the scientific world to harness this incredible force.

At another time, Benjamin was having problems with his vision. He had two pairs of glasses, one to help his see things far away and anther for seeing things that were close up. But it became tiresome to always switch back and forth between the two pairs of glasses, so Franklin decided to try and experiment.

Very carefully, Franklin cut the glass lenses from each pair in half. He then glued the top half of the distant lenses onto the bottom half of the close up lenses, and then he could use just one pair of glasses for seeing things both close up and far away. This was the first pair of what we now call "bifocal" lenses, and nowadays millions of people around the world use them.

Ben Franklin was also interested in the weather. During one especially intense storm, he paid close attention to which way the wind was blowing. Being in Philadelphia, about 300 miles away from Boston, Franklin realized that he could learn a lot about the movement of large storms by talking to someone in Boston about how the storm looked when it passed over their city. To his surprise, Franklin learned that even though the wind seemed to be blowing in the direction of Boston, the storm never reached them. He had just taken the first step towards understanding global winds (in this case, the Gulf Stream) and how they affected storm movement.

Franklin even invented swim fins, which allow divers to conserve energy as they move through the water.

Even though he had to leave school when he was just ten years old, there was no doubt that Franklin had taken advantage of all the information available to him to educate himself as much as he could. Recognizing his high level of intelligence and how much he had contributed to the world, Franklin eventually received honorary degrees from several respected universities, including Harvard, Yale, and Oxford.

Chapter 3: The Late Life of Benjamin Franklin

In 1757, something exciting happened – the state of Pennsylvania asked Benjamin Franklin, one of their most prominent and respected citizens, to speak for them in England. Although the Thirteen Colonies could not officially vote on any new laws that might affect them, they were allowed to send citizens to London to try and explain American opinions to important voting members of Parliament. Ben Franklin was one of those citizens sent to London.

His wife, Deborah, was afraid of making such a long trip by boat, so she stayed back in Philadelphia and took care of their home. She and Benjamin wrote lots of letters to each other, often talking about how much they missed each other.

Benjamin Franklin was respected by those he worked with in London. Everyone knew that he was a hard worker, had a good sense of humor, and was intelligent. When things got tense between the American colonies and England, Ben Franklin was often able to be the voice of reason and to calm things down.

For example, in 1765 the English Parliament passed a unpopular law that affected the American colonies. In order to get the tax money used to pay the English soldiers who had fought in the French and Indian War, Parliament passed the Stamp Act of 1765. How did this law affect the daily lives of American colonists? It required the colonists to use special "stamped" paper for official documents, newspapers, and magazines. The colonists could only buy this paper only from the English and could only do so using English money.

The colonists were not happy with this law as it forced them to pay money for something that they didn't feel that they needed. One of the first in a series of laws that placed heavy taxes on the colonists, the Americans complained that they were experiencing "taxation without representation". In other words, because no American could vote on new laws, they felt that they were being treated more as slaves than citizens.

For all of his life, Benjamin Franklin had been proud to be English. He loved the culture and the humor, the proud history and the strong economy of his birth nation. But since he had arrived in London, his viewpoint of the English way of governing began to change. From 1757 to 1775, he had lived in London and acted as a voice for several colonies, including Pennsylvania, Georgia, New Jersey, and Massachusetts. But in that time he had seen that English politics was largely corrupt.

In his own way, Ben Franklin tried to bring out the worst politicians and make them face justice. Around the time that the Stamp Act was passed and Americans began to complain about the heavy taxes,

Franklin did something rash, and for which he was severely and publically disciplined – he released a series of confidential letters written by Massachusetts Governor Thomas Hutchinson. The letters showed that he was actually encouraging the English crown to crack down on the residents of Boston and to take away more of their freedom. The letters made the people of Boston even angrier and got Benjamin Franklin in lots of trouble.

Franklin strongly opposed the Stamp Act, helped to repeal it, and protested other unfair tax laws passed by Parliament. As events such as the Boston Massacre and the Boston Tea Party heated up the situation back in America, Benjamin Franklin realized that things were coming to a head. He was being forced to choose sides in a situation where he felt loyalty and compassion for both sides. He had been born an English citizen and was proud to be a part of the British Empire, but he had been raised in America and wanted to make sure that his fellow Americans weren't mistreated by the English crown.

The more he thought about the situation and about how corrupt English politicians were, the more he realized that Americans could never change the way that Parliament made decisions and treated their colonies. The only way for Americans to be truly free would be to rebel against the English and to fight for their independence.

Way back in 1754, Franklin had given some thought about how the Thirteen Colonies could become independent, and what sort of government and laws they should have. After the Stamp Act of 1765 was passed, Franklin once again began to work on his ideas for American Independence. By about 1775, it was clear that England did not want to respect the American colonists, so Benjamin Franklin went back home to Philadelphia and together with Thomas Jefferson and others prepared the wording of the Declaration of Independence.

By this time, Franklin's wife Deborah had died. His daughter Sally was married, and his son William was a prominent politician. But as the American War for Independence grew closer, it became clear that father and son had different ideas about which was the best course to take. While Benjamin was convinced that the right thing to do was to fight for independence, William was firm in his loyalty to the English crown. A deep division began to separate the two family members, and the wounds never truly healed.

Although Thomas Jefferson wrote the actual Declaration of Independence, much of the ideas and wording came from Benjamin Franklin's mind. He was part of the small committee that put the final touches on the document, and he was one of the signers of it. Also, he helped to write The Articles of Confederation, which were eventually approved by all Thirteen Colonies by 1781, two years before the Revolutionary War ended.

One of the most important features of the Articles of Confederation was the importance given to "state's rights". According to article two of the Articles of Confederation:

"Each state retains its sovereignty, freedom,
and independence, and every power,
jurisdiction, and right, which is not by this
Confederation expressly delegated to the
United States, in Congress assembled."[10]

The Articles of Confederation made the state
government the most important power in the United
States. This made a lot of the colonists happy. Instead
of being bossed around by a large central power, as
had been the case with England, the power would stay
in the hands of smaller local governments.
And according to article three of the Articles of
Confederation, there would be a special relationship
between the states:

"The said States hereby severally enter into a
firm league of friendship with each other, for
their common defense, the security of their
liberties, and their mutual and general welfare,
binding themselves to assist each other,
against all force offered to, or attacks made
upon them, or any of them, on account of
religion, sovereignty, trade, or any other
pretense whatever."[11]

Under the new articles, there would be a "Continental
Congress", which was a group of representatives from
each state who would get together to talk and to make
important decisions for the new country people.

[10]   Articles   of   Confederation   source:
http://avalon.law.yale.edu/18th_century/artconf.asp#art2

[11]   Articles   of   Confederation   source:
http://avalon.law.yale.edu/18th_century/artconf.asp#art2

Congress could declare war and peace, send and receive ambassadors to and from foreign countries, and appoint officers for the army in times of war. A President of the Congress would be appointed to call meetings and coordinate them. Money would never be demanded from the states, only requested.

These Articles gave the early Americans a much different life than they had had under the British way of doing things. They were finally free to make their own decisions, to have a voice in their government, and to have real allies (political friends) that they could count on when times got tough. Benjamin Franklin's ideas and confidence in the American people heavily influenced these articles.

After having helped to write the Declaration of Independence and the Articles of Confederation, Benjamin Franklin again travelled to Europe to represent America. But instead of going back to London, Franklin was sent to Paris to try and get the help of the French government. Franklin stayed in Paris until 1785. During that time, he did a lot to help the colonists win the war against England. His charming personality and good reputation helped to convince the French government that America was worth fighting for. Franklin was even invited to spend time in the court of King Louis XVI, something that few people were ever invited to do.

In Paris, Franklin also spent quite a lot of time with women. Because he was now a single man again, he was often seen with different women having dinner and laughing. In fact, he even proposed to one wealthy widow, but she rejected him.

By 1778, Franklin had done much to help win French support, which included important loans to the colonists. By the time the war had come to a close, he was one of the representatives of the new American government who signed the Treaty of Paris in 1783, officially bringing an end to the war.

The document was signed on September 3, 1783 and had several important points[12], but perhaps the most important was the first one: the United States would be free, sovereign and independent states.

From that moment on the United States would be recognized as independent, and the British government would have to respect them.

[13]

In 1785, Franklin returned to the United States, to Philadelphia, and Thomas Jefferson took his place as Ambassador to France. Back in America, Franklin was treated as a kind of celebrity. Everywhere he

---

[12]   Full   document   text   source:
http://www.ourdocuments.gov/doc.php?doc=6&page=transcript

[13]   Image:
http://revolution.mrdonn.org/the%20treaty%20of%20Paris.jpg

went crowds formed, and everyone wanted to shake the hand of the man who had done so much for both his country and for the entire world. He had helped the scientific community to move forward, had helped an entire country to gain its independence, and he had helped a generation of young men to use their minds to thinks clearly and to find solutions for problems.

By this time, Franklin was 79 years old. He suffered from a disease called "gout" which caused his foot to swell and even made walking painful. He didn't travel as much anymore and tended to stay close to home with his daughter sally and her family. Despite his age, however, Franklin would make two more important contributions to the United States before his death.

The first of his final two actions on behalf of America came in the spring of 1787. For more than ten years, the Articles of Confederation that Franklin himself had helped to write had governed the way that decisions were made, and things were done in the young country. But the Articles of Confederation, while definitely better than life under English rule, still had lots of problems.

For example, because each state got one vote and thirteen unanimous votes were needed to make any kind of change to the Articles, it meant that nothing really ever got done. For example, if the smallest state – Rhode Island – didn't like a particular decision that everyone did, meaning the majority of Americans, they could block the new law. It wasn't long before people started to look at the Articles as a silly set of laws that didn't deserve any respect. The new government couldn't even get the money it needed to pay soldiers from the revolutionary War, which even led to some civil problems in Massachusetts.

A convention was called to fix the problems with the Articles, and Benjamin Franklin was invited to join it. From May to September of 1787, he and other important Americans (including George Washington and James Madison) sat together in a hot and stuffy room to decide how the government should be organized. But instead of simply fixing the Articles of Confederation, the men wrote and signed an entirely new constitution, the same one that is used by the United States Government today.

Among the important decisions made during this "Constitutional Convention", it was decided that there would be two houses of Congress, one with equal representation and one with representation based on population. It was decided to leave slavery alone for the moment and to include a Bill of Rights to guarantee certain freedoms to every American. Benjamin Franklin happily signed the new set of laws.

The new constitution was a fair and balanced document, and over the years changes have been made as necessary. But the one thing that the constitution didn't talk a lot about – slavery - was what really bothered Franklin in his final days. He couldn't stand the idea that American soldiers had fought and died for the idea that every person was free to decide how to live his life, only to see millions of African-Americans living in forced servitude.

Although the laws about slavery would be changed decades later, during the time of the American Civil War, Franklin decided to publish some of his final writings on the subject of abolition – ending slavery. He even served as the President of the Pennsylvania Abolitionist Society.

Finally, this historic man's life came to an end. On April 17, 1790, Benjamin Franklin died at his daughter Sally's house. He never really made peace with his son, who had moved to England and started a family there.

At his funeral, more than 20,000 people showed up to pay their respects.

Conclusion

The influence of Benjamin Franklin is still felt every day in the United States. His ideas helped to write the laws that govern us today. His curious spirit helped to create the technology we use daily. And his desire for liberty – for both White and African Americans, helped to shape a truly revolutionary idea of freedom for all, no matter how much money or education they had or the color of their skin.

Today, many people think of Franklin flying a kite in a storm or see his face on a $100 bill.

14

But he did so much more than that. His wisdom is still repeated almost 250 years after his death, and the things he did to improve life in Philadelphia – set up a

14   Image: http://www.loasite.com/wp-content/uploads/2013/01/100-dollar-bill.jpg

library, a volunteer fire department, and fire insurance – are still things that make life better for Americans everywhere.

For many reasons, Benjamin Franklin is often considered the "first" American. He was one of the first people to demonstrate the ideals and qualities that the Founding Fathers hoped would come to define this young nation. And over the years, many have followed in Franklin's footsteps. Think of the NASA scientists who sent men to the moon, of Civil Rights leaders like Martin Luther King Jr., or forward-thinking politicians like Franklin Delano Roosevelt.

Franklin also left behind a legacy that every person should "pay it forward". In other words, each American should take some of the good things they have received and pass them on to others. Modern day examples of those who "pay it forward" include Bill and Melinda Gates, who have used the large amount of money earned through their business to start educational and other charities all over the world, helping not only Americans but people born on the other side of the Earth.

Benjamin Franklin once said:

> "If you would not be forgotten, as soon as you are dead and buried, either write things worth reading, or do things worth the writing"[15].

---

[15] Quotation:

Franklin himself did both. He wrote fascination commentaries on society and science worth reading and did enough things to fill a whole shelf of interesting books. He wasn't afraid to make mistakes or to get things wrong. It was more important for him to keep on moving forward, to keep growing and progressing. He wanted to learn more and to use what he learned to make the lives of those around him better and better. A real pioneer of American industry, Benjamin Franklin stands tall as an example for all humans, not just Americans, to imitate.

Made in the USA
Monee, IL
10 February 2023